WAR OF THE GIANT ROBOTS!

Earth has been invaded by the powerful
robots from the distant planet Cybertron
– the Heroic Autobots and their enemies,
the Evil Decepticons. They can disguise
their robot shapes as earthly machines
and transform for battle at lightning
speed. The battle between Good and Evil
rages on Earth . . .

MEGATRON, the Evil Decepticon
leader, is plotting to seize a huge haul of
microchips with which to build a mighty
army. But his arch-foe, Autobot chief
OPTIMUS PRIME, is out to stop him.
On this terrible battle depends the future
of the world . . .

THE TRANSFORMERS™

ADVENTURE GAME BOOKS

Highway Clash

Also published by Young Corgi Books

THE TRANSFORMERS®

Highway Clash

Dave Morris
Illustrated by John Higgins

YOUNG CORGI BOOKS

THE TRANSFORMERS™:
HIGHWAY CLASH

A YOUNG CORGI BOOK 0 552 52317 8

PRINTING HISTORY
Young Corgi edition published 1986
Reprinted 1986

Young Corgi Books are published by Transworld
Publishers Ltd., 61–63 Uxbridge Road, Ealing,
London W5 5SA, in Australia by Transworld
Publishers (Australia) Pty. Ltd., 15-23 Helles
Avenue, Moorebank, NSW 2170, and in New Zealand
by Transworld Publishers (N.Z.) Ltd., Cnr. Moselle
and Waipareira Avenues, Henderson, Auckland.

Made and printed in Great Britain by the
Guernsey Press Co. Ltd., Guernsey, Channel Islands.

This is an adventure story. But it is not like most other adventure stories – there is one big difference.

You are the main character.

What happens in the story depends on **your** decisions. The fate of The Transformers – whether OPTIMUS PRIME will win the day or whether the evil plans of MEGATRON will succeed – is in **your** hands.

Do not read the pages of this adventure in numerical order, as you would an ordinary book. You should start at page **1**, of course, but where you go to from there will depend on what you choose to do.

Prepare yourself to meet The Transformers!

NOW TURN TO PAGE **1**. . .

The Yorkshire Dales can be a bleak place in winter, but in summer they are great for a camping holiday. This warm, sunny morning you are sitting with your back to a very ancient granite block (known locally as the Druid Stone). You came out with a drawing-pad, intending to sketch the nearby reservoir, but you feel too lazy for that. You sit back and enjoy the sunshine.

Hearing a rumble in the distance you turn your head, hoping that it is not thunder. Luckily, there is hardly a cloud in the sky. The noise you heard is a huge lorry that is slowly trundling along the road a few kilometres away. It must be carrying delicate cargo if it has to move that slowly. It must be valuable as well, because it is escorted by a police car and several motorcycles. You are about to return to your daydream when the sun glints off something shiny in the grass nearby.

If you want to investigate this, turn to page **2**
If you ignore it and go on lazing in the sun, turn to page **19**

1

You are very disappointed because nothing happens straightaway. You are about to give up when you hear a strange humming from under your feet. The steel door slides back to reveal a metal ramp that leads down into the earth. You nervously walk down it – keeping an eye on the door behind you. You want to be ready to run back out if it suddenly starts to close.

The ramp leads into a weird underground hideaway. It looks like something out of *Star Wars* – a maze of metal corridors and winking lights. Then you think you can make out voices. They sound electronic – not human!

If you want to go left, towards the voices, turn to page **4**
If you want to go right, turn to page **6**

You walk quickly along the corridor and enter a large control room. Flashing computer panels and bleeping instruments cover the walls. You look around for a moment then start to back away into the corridor. You are startled by a movement – there are two figures you had not noticed at first. They are large, oddly shaped and mechanical. You mistook them for pieces of machinery. Now that they are moving, you recognize that they are robot warriors! One of them is a real giant. He towers up to the ceiling, armoured in silver and blue-grey with a powerful cannon along his right arm. Even the smaller robot is bigger than you are. His armour is black and red and he carries a bright steel rifle.

If you make a run for it, turn to page **7**
If you decide to try talking to them, turn to page **8**

5

You move away from the voices. For a minute you cannot hear them, then you pass a grating and hear them clearly again. The grating is loose, so you remove it and squeeze through into the room beyond. It is a vast control room filled with humming computers and flickering display screens. Two robot warriors stand in the room. Even the smaller of them is more than twice your size. He is red and black and holds a silver rifle at his side. The other, a silver and blue-grey giant with a mighty cannon on his arm, is obviously the leader. You are hidden from view behind a projecting beam, so they have not noticed you yet.

If you speak to them, turn to page **8**
If you stay hidden and listen to what they're saying, turn to page **9**
If you make your way outside again, turn to page **13**

They are after you! You run back to the surface and away from the steel door. You press the button as you dash past, but it does not close. The robots' heavy footsteps echo up from the open tunnel. You can hear the giant robot snarling orders in his harsh voice. Then a high-pitched whine starts up which sounds unpleasantly like a dentist's drill. You look around in desperation.

Will you hide behind the Druid Stone? If so, turn to page 10
If you keep running, turn to page 12

'Hello,' says the giant robot. 'I am OPTIMUS PRIME, leader of the Heroic Autobots, and this is my assistant PROWL. Do not be alarmed. Despite our terrifying appearance we are on the side of you Earthlings. Watch.' He turns to activate a video screen and you see a view of the road outside. The lorry is still inching along it. 'That truck is carrying vital electronic equipment. The Evil Decepticons – our enemies – want it, and we are sure they'll stop at nothing. We are here to protect the lorry and its cargo. Will you help us, Earthling?'

If you refuse to help, turn to page **14**
If you agree, turn to page **16**

The giant robot gestures for his companion to switch on a video screen. Craning your neck, you see that the screen shows a view of the road above. The lorry you noticed before is still trundling along it, guarded by the police escort.

'You see, mighty MEGATRON,' whines the smaller robot. 'It is as I said – the Autobots are already secretly guarding the microchips.'

'Be silent, RUMBLE!' thunders the giant robot. 'Your endless chattering disturbs my logic circuits. I must plan an attack that leaves nothing to chance.'

As MEGATRON thinks about his plan, you retreat into the main corridor. You had better get out of here before you are spotted. You hastily return to the exit.

Turn to page **13**

The smaller robot comes out from the underground hideout just as you take cover. The grating whine you can hear is coming from his sonic rifle. He looks around but does not see you.

'The Earthling has escaped me, great MEGATRON,' he calls down through the doorway. 'Shall I use my sensors to locate it?'

'No, let it go,' replies a deep voice. 'And get back down here before the Autobots see you!'

You wait until you hear the steel door clang shut before emerging from behind the Druid Stone. What can MEGATRON have meant by his last remark? No-one is nearby except for the police and lorry-driver more than a mile away.

Turn to page **13**

The smaller robot steps through the doorway. The whining noise is coming from his sonic rifle. Looking over your shoulder as you run, you see him taking aim. You reckon that he cannot be a very good shot. The rifle is not pointing anywhere near you. You keep running, sure that you have a good chance of getting away.

Suddenly a blast of sound comes from the rifle and causes a rippling vibration in the earth. It spreads along the ground and causes a small earth tremor right below your feet! The next thing you know, the robot has picked you up and is carrying you back underground to the control room where his leader waits. 'I could have killed you if I'd wanted,' he says.

Turn to page **8**

A roar splits the sky like a sonic boom. A huge flying cannon thunders overhead towards the road, unleashing dazzling anti-matter blasts as it goes. The police are thrown into confusion. There is nothing they can do against this attack. But then you see the police car beginning to change shape. The driver leaps out as his vehicle becomes a tall robot which gleams white and black in the midday sun. The lorry-driver is also getting out of his cab with an astonished look on his face as his own vehicle transforms into a giant blue-and-red robot carrying a laser rifle!

'Clear the area!' the giant robot is calling to the startled police. 'I, OPTIMUS PRIME, and my assistant, PROWL, can survive our enemy's attacks – but you frail humans cannot. Ughh – !' He is thrown back by a direct hit from the cannon. Suddenly the giant robot you saw earlier, appears. The barrel of the giant cannon moves to his command. His smaller accomplice is also closing to attack.

'MEGATRON – as I expected,' shouts OPTIMUS PRIME, 'And you have RUMBLE with you!'

'We shall see who can survive our attacks, OPTIMUS,' chortles MEGATRON as his foe gets up.

Turn to page **26**

The larger robot turns his back on you. You are no longer of any interest to him. 'Take this Earthling worm away, RUMBLE,' he snarls.

'At once, imperial MEGATRON!' replies the smaller robot gleefully, seizing your arm before you can run. He half drags and half carries you to a barred cell. Standing in front of the cell, he levels his sonic rifle at a switch by the door. The door slides open in response to a high-pitched tone, and RUMBLE shoves you roughly inside before closing the bars with another sonic command. 'You will rot here forever, human,' he sneers, then returns to report to MEGATRON.

Turn to page **20**

'Good,' says the robot who calls himself OPTIMUS PRIME. 'Here is our plan. The microchips the lorry is transporting are very valuable to the Decepticons. They wouldn't have any trouble with the human police guarding the lorry at the moment, but we know they won't dare attack *us*. Logically, we should take the microchips and deliver them safely to their destination. I'd prefer to explain things to the police, of course, but we realized they wouldn't trust us.'

'They'd just think we're the Decepticons,' says the smaller robot.

'We want you to stop the convoy and explain things to the police, so they won't be alarmed when they see us.' He starts to escort you to the surface. 'I see the lorry is moving quite slowly – these microchips are very delicate. You'll have no trouble stopping it.'

'But be quick about it, kid,' yells the smaller robot as you hurry off. You don't like people calling you 'kid'.

Turn to page **17**

The convoy is indeed moving very slowly. The highway has some sharp bends around here, and obviously the microchips could be damaged if a crate fell over inside the lorry. As you approach the road, you begin to have second thoughts about this. Should you really stop the police and start telling them about giant robot warriors? Will they believe you? And were the robots telling the truth anyway?

If you decide to go ahead and stop the convoy, turn to page 18
If you give up and walk away, turn to page 29

You step out into the road a few hundred metres ahead of the convoy and start waving your arms frantically. They see you, and the police car speeds ahead to see what you want. It pulls up. The policeman inside is just getting out when suddenly there is a loud rumble and the road breaks apart under your feet. You and the policeman are flung to the ground and you see him hit his head. The convoy is being attacked by the two robots who claimed to be friendly. The smaller one is sending shockwaves through the ground with his sonic rifle while his master hurls cannon-blasts to scatter the motorcycle police.

Then you see something happening to the police car and the lorry. They are beginning to alter shape, changing shape into two more robot fighters!

Turn to page **25**

You are gazing at the reservoir glimmering in the sunlight, daydreaming about starships, wizards and galactic empires, when a loud roar makes you sit up with a jolt. Over on the road, you are astonished to see the convoy being attacked by two robot warriors. One – a giant with a cannon built on to his right arm – is scattering the terrified policeman with antimatter blasts. 'Quickly, RUMBLE,' he calls to his smaller accomplice. 'Let us take what we want and waste no time here.'

'Yes, great MEGATRON!' replies the other. He sees the lorry-driver scrambling out of his cab, and throws him off his feet with a sonic pulse that cracks the road surface. However, as he strides triumphantly towards the abandoned lorry he begins to hesitate. The lorry is changing shape – and so is the police car. They transform into two gleaming robots who stand ready to challenge the Evil Decepticons.

'OPTIMUS PRIME and PROWL!' gasps MEGATRON.

Turn to page **26**

You wait in the cramped cell until you hear the clang of the outer door. You know that the two robots have left. You are alone in the control complex, and your thoughts turn towards finding a way out. Searching your pockets, you find a paperclip which you straighten out. Perhaps you could pick the lock with it. Alternatively, you could try to whistle the tone that RUMBLE used to open the bars.

If you try to pick the lock, turn to page **21**
If you try imitating the sound that opens the door, turn to page **22**
If you just wait where you are, turn to page **23**

You twist the end of the wire and insert it into the lock. You have seen this done in films, but you find now that it is not as easy you thought. You twist the wire around, but all you succeed in doing is breaking off the tip. The Evil Decepticons could be back at any moment. Will you try again to pick the lock?

If you do, turn to page **23**
If you try to whistle the exact note that opens the bars, turn to page **22**

You start to whistle a high note and gradually make it louder and more high-pitched. Suddenly the switch beside the cell gives a click and the bars open to release you. Success! RUMBLE never imagined you would be able to imitate the note that opens the door. He probably forgot that youngsters have a wider range of hearing than adults and assumed you couldn't even hear the sound.

You return to the empty control room. MEGATRON has left a video screen on, showing a view of the road outside. The convoy is under attack from evil MEGATRON and his snivelling assistant RUMBLE. But even as you watch, you see the lorry changing shape to become a robot as big as MEGATRON, and the police car alters to become a white-and-black warrior with fierce red eyes. They are fighting to stop MEGATRON stealing the shipment of microchips. From what you hear over the speaker, you realize that the two newcomers are the *real* OPTIMUS PRIME and PROWL!

If you run up to the surface where the battle is taking place, turn to page **26**
If you prefer to stay here and try to use some of MEGATRON's devices against him, turn to page **28**

You are still waiting in the cell about ten minutes later when the robots return. They are crowing over a victory. 'Magnificent MEGATRON!' yelps RUMBLE. 'As usual, your plans have been a total success. The Autobots never knew what hit them.'

You hear MEGATRON's frighteningly deep voice ordering RUMBLE to carry something into the control room. His words crackle with static – whatever battle they have just won, the Decepticons obviously did not come out of it completely uninjured. RUMBLE limps up to your cell. The paintwork on his armour is bubbled and blackened as though he has been in a fire. When he sees you looking at this, he sneers: 'Decepticons are trained to fight however bad their injuries. And now, human, it is time to end your worthless life.' He produces a shrill note from his sonic cannon which causes the bars to slide apart, then he reaches for you. However, before he can drag you out of the cell, MEGATRON's merciless voice calls out, summoning RUMBLE to him. RUMBLE grunts in annoyance and strides off, closing the bars as he goes.

The bars are sliding together again, but they have not closed yet. If you are quick, you may be able to leap between them before they do. It may be your one chance to escape – but dare you risk it?

If you jump through the closing cell door, turn to page 52

If you play safe and stay in the cell, turn to page 54

As the lorry-driver jumps from his cab, it is transforming itself to become a giant robot. The police car changes too. The men who were driving these vehicles are obviously as astonished as you are. A cannon-blast from the robot who claimed to be friendly, sends the giant newcomer sprawling. When the police-robot calls out in concern you realize that these two, who were secretly guarding the convoy, are the *real* OPTIMUS PRIME and PROWL. Then the other two must have tricked you!

PROWL is trying to get a clear shot at his giant enemy, but has to move because you are in the way. 'RUMBLE,' calls the evil robot as he tears the doors from the lorry, 'collect what we want while I see to our enemies!'

'At once, great MEGATRON,' replies the smaller robot. He removes a crate from the back of the lorry while MEGATRON sends out a barrage of cannon-bursts. OPTIMUS, still reeling from the sneak attack, is thrown from the road. PROWL cannot fight back as he has to shield you from the deadly blasts. He too is flung back, stunned, as MEGATRON and RUMBLE flee the scene with the stolen microchips.

Turn to page **38**

MEGATRON sends OPTIMUS PRIME reeling with a titanic cannon-blast, but the Autobot quickly recovers and responds with searing laser-shots. However, he does not notice RUMBLE, who sneaks hurriedly around to the abandoned trailer and tears off the doors. PROWL runs to stop him from stealing the valuable cargo, but is knocked off his feet and stunned by a shot in the back from MEGATRON's fearsome cannon.

'Take the microchips to safety, RUMBLE,' shouts MEGATRON in a chilling voice. '*I* shall deal with the Autobots.'

RUMBLE tucks a crate under his arm and starts running from the road. The hidden door to the Decepticon hideout lies in the bushes just beyond the Druid Stone. He glances over his shoulder to the road. Thick plumes of smoke and dazzling bomb-bursts mean that the Autobots have lost sight of him. In a moment he will have disappeared into the hideout. Dare you try and stop him?

If you stand by the Druid Stone and yell at RUMBLE, turn to page **34**
If you run towards the reservoir, turn to page **36**
If you stay hidden where you are, turn to page **33**

You scan the bewildering number of flickering instruments – switches, dials, display screens and buttons. You have no idea what they do, and you will have to rely on guesswork. After a while, you settle on three possible instruments that you decide might be of some use. Which will you try:

A red-handled lever? Turn to page **31**
A grey switch? Turn to page **32**
A green button? Turn to page **30**

28

You shrug and walk away, but you have not gone far before a deafening roar throws you to the ground. The robots you saw earlier go charging past towards the road, where the convoy has already spotted them and halted in confusion. 'Bah! Treacherous Earthlet,' says the smaller robot as he passes you. 'I would punish you for disobedience if I had the time –'

'Come, RUMBLE,' calls the giant robot as he approaches the convoy. 'Waste no further time with your prattling!'

The smaller robot glowers at you and goes to assist his leader. They *were* lying after all, then – they planned to steal the convoy's shipment all along.

The police soon see they can do nothing against these two unearthly robots, and run for cover. But as the lorry-driver scrambles out of his cab, it begins to change shape. The police car is changing shape, too – and from the looks on their faces, the policemen are as surprised as you are. The two vehicles are soon replaced by two mighty robots. These two are not in league with the others, however, for they begin to use their own weapons to protect the valuable shipment.

'Oh mighty MEGATRON,' whines RUMBLE. 'It is as we suspected – OPTIMUS PRIME and PROWL anticipated our plan!'

Turn to page **26**

The instant you pull the lever, all the lights in the room go out. Red emergency lamps come on in their place, and a warning siren begins to blare. You have a definite feeling that you should leave, as you cannot switch off the siren by reversing the lever. Running for the door, you begin to worry that you might not be able to open it, but luckily it swings aside automatically as you rush up the ramp and into the open air. As you stumble away, you are horrified to see that RUMBLE is only about twenty metres away – and heading in your direction! He has a crate under his arm. When he sees you he sets it down carefully on the grass. You start to run towards the road, but RUMBLE only laughs. 'You cannot escape now, Earthling!'

OPTIMUS PRIME and PROWL are locked in battle with MEGATRON. They have not noticed your danger, and are too far off to help you anyway. RUMBLE aims his rifle at you . . .

*Turn to page **37***

You flick the switch. All that happens is that the video screen goes blank. You turn the switch again and it comes back on. Rather disappointing, you think – but perhaps it is better not to meddle with these strange alien devices. You might blow the whole place sky-high!

On the video screen, you see that RUMBLE has ransacked the lorry's cargo and is making off with a crate. The valiant Autobots are still battling MEGATRON, but they are hampered by their concern for the innocent humans nearby and it looks as if the Decepticon leader is getting the upper hand. RUMBLE is obviously coming back to the hideout, and you wonder if you have time to leave before he gets here.

If you leave now, turn to page **44**
If you try to hide somewhere, turn to page **45**

You watch RUMBLE scurry down into the underground hideout. Meanwhile, on the road, PROWL has managed to get all the policemen clear. OPTIMUS PRIME now has no need to worry about hurting innocent bystanders and is able to use the full power of his laser against MEGATRON. You watch in awe. Who will win – the valiant leader of the Autobots, or his evil and ruthless foe?

Suddenly MEGATRON abandons the battle and takes to the air. Sending down a barrage of cannon-bursts to cover his retreat, he streaks through the air. He is out of sight of the road and hidden by a bank when he returns to the hideout. You saw where he went, but the Autobots did not.

Turn to page **38**

RUMBLE turns with a distinct scowl on his metal face. 'Why, you meddlesome brat,' he murmurs menacingly. 'You'll not trouble me again!' He raises his sonic rifle, ready to send bone-shattering shockwaves through the ground towards you.

You see the earth ripple like waves on a shore as the shockwave rides towards you. But as it meets the firm foundation of the Druid Stone a remarkable thing happens – the shockwave bounces back. You are flung aside unhurt, but the wave has doubled in intensity by the time it returns to the Decepticon who sent it. He tries too slowly to turn off his sonic rifle, and is catapulted off his feet as the ground splits under him.

Turn to page **39**

RUMBLE sees you and cries out in rage. 'I'll see to you, Earth brat, before I do anything else –'

You are running up the steep bank to the reservoir, but it is a hard climb. Out of breath, you turn round and see that RUMBLE has pointed his sonic rifle at you. 'You're going to see first-hand why they call me RUMBLE, kid,' he growls. He is adjusting the setting on his rifle. 'I'm going for *maximum intensity*!'

You screw your eyes shut as you feel the low-frequency soundwaves shaking the air around you. The reservoir wall is shuddering under the onslaught. Things look bleak for you, but you will not give up yet. You clamber a bit further up the bank, and just then the reservoir wall splits apart! Clinging to the bank, you are delighted to see RUMBLE swept off his feet by a powerful flood of water.

Turn to page **39**

A deafening explosion splits the ground and a huge pillar of flame and smoke erupts from the open doorway into the Decepticons' liar. You are thrown on to your back, which knocks the breath out of your lungs but leaves you otherwise unhurt. RUMBLE is not so lucky. Caught in the edge of the blast, he is thrown several metres and seems to be dazed. The lever you pulled was obviously some kind of self-destruct device!

Turn to page **39**

Following the Decepticon attack, several policemen lie groaning. It is a miracle that no-one was killed, but many were injured by flying rocks when MEGATRON shattered the road with his cannon-blasts.

OPTIMUS PRIME orders PROWL to revert to his car-form. He and Roller, OPTIMUS's transit-module, must take the wounded to hospital. OPTIMUS PRIME turns to you. 'We must recover the vital microchips the Decepticons stole,' he says. 'They can be used to build intelligent computers. We were secretly guarding them because we knew MEGATRON might try to steal them. He wants them so that he can create more robots to add to his Decepticon army!'

You see there is no time to waste. You show OPTIMUS where you saw the Decepticons vanish into their underground lair.

Turn to page 55

While RUMBLE struggles to recover, you run over to where he left the crate he took from the lorry. Printed on the side is a label: *Computer microchips – handle with extreme care.* One of the planks in the side of the crate has got broken, and the delicate silicon chips are spilling out of their packing.

There is a low roar in the sky. MEGATRON, now transformed into a massive flying cannon, is bearing down on you. 'Stand away from that crate, human!' he thunders, his voice crackling with rage. You glance towards the road. The Autobots are coming this way, but they will get here too late to help you. Everything is in your hands now!

If you leave the crate and run, turn to page **42**
If you try to drag the crate, turn to page **41**
If you threaten to smash the microchips, turn to page **40**

'Okay, MEGATRON,' you shout. 'Attack me – that's if you want your precious microchips destroyed!' You throw a handful of chips on to the ground and hold your foot over them. Seeing you ready to crush the precious chips, MEGATRON hesitates. The delay buys you the few moments needed for the Autobots to arrive. PROWL sends a steel fist flying against RUMBLE, who has just got to his feet only to be knocked down again. OPTIMUS PRIME closes with the evil MEGATRON for a clash of robot titans!

Turn to page **56**

The crate is very heavy. You try to drag it, but have to give up. MEGATRON is hovering overhead. He dare not shoot for fear of destroying the microchips he wants so badly. A steel-shod hand seizes your leg – RUMBLE has recovered. Fortunately the delay has bought you the few moments needed for the Autobots to arrive on the scene. A powerful blow from PROWL sends RUMBLE sprawling, while OPTIMUS PRIME closes with his arch-foe MEGATRON.

Turn to page **56**

You have a horrible idea as you run for the exit. What if you cannot get the door open from inside? Luckily it swings back automatically as you approach, and you run up the ramp into the open air. RUMBLE is running towards you with the crate under his arm. His leader is still occupied fighting the Autobots. What will you do?

If you hide, turn to page **33**
If you stand by the Druid Stone and yell at RUMBLE, turn to page **34**
If you run towards the reservoir, turn to page **36**

44

You decide to conceal yourself in a cupboard off the main control room. You acted not a moment too soon, because you soon hear RUMBLE enter. Peering out into the room, you discover that he is standing right by the door of the cupboard where you are hiding! Luckily he has his back to you. You pull the door shut after making sure that it has a handle on the inside. Heavy metal footsteps tell you that MEGATRON has entered as well.

'Look at the viewscreen, RUMBLE,' chortles the Decepticon leader. 'The Autobots did not see us enter this base – they must think we've vanished into empty air!'

'As ever, your cunning and strength are victorious, great leader,' replies RUMBLE. He is still standing next to your hiding-place.

'Bah, you toady!' growls MEGATRON. 'Attend to the microchips. See that they are properly packed. I will have your parts for scrap if a single component is damaged!'

Stepping back against the wall of the cupboard, you find several strange instruments. Possibly you could use one of them to attack the Decepticons – but it would undoubtedly be safer just to hide here for the time being.

If you use one of the instruments, turn to page **46**
If you just wait in hiding, turn to page **48**

In the glimmer of light under the cupboard door, you examine the items you have found. There is a curious ray-projector labelled an 'anti-matter converter', a roll of silvered metal foil and a box of ball bearings. Which will you try to use against the Decepticons:

The ball bearings? Turn to page **49**
The anti-matter converter? Turn to page **50**
The silvered foil? Turn to page **51**

You huddle back into the cupboard and wait. After what seems like hours, you hear the sound of metal-shod feet crossing the control-room floor. 'The Autobots are searching several miles away, commander.' RUMBLE's voice.

'Good. We shall depart.'

You emerge from the cupboard when you are sure they've gone. Climbing the ramp, you reach the surface and see a bright pinpoint of light streaking away through the sky. The Evil Decepticons have escaped with their prize, and so this is

THE END

You summon up all your courage and step out of your hiding-place. The Decepticons look round at you in astonishment – they had forgotten all about you.

'What!' screams MEGATRON. 'Seize this Earth creature, RUMBLE.'

RUMBLE rushes forward eagerly, arms spread wide to catch you. You surprise him by not turning to run. You just pour the ball bearings out of their box on to the floor in front of him. He slips, arms flailing in a desperate attempt to keep his balance, then falls heavily on his back with a crash.

MEGATRON strides forward. You think it might be time to run now. Under his massive feet, the ball bearings only crack like popcorn.

Just as MEGATRON is reaching down to grab you, a harsh sound echoes through the room. It sounds as if someone just tore off the outer door of the hideout.

'The Autobots –' says MEGATRON. 'They've found us.'

Turn to page **57**

The Decepticons had forgotten all about you, and are startled to see you step out of the cupboard with the ray-projector in your hands.

'You troublesome Earth-creature!' cries MEGA-TRON. 'I shall stop your meddling right now.'

He levels his massive cannon at you. With nothing to lose, you click the switch on the side of the anti-matter converter and it bathes MEGATRON in an eerie blue light. His cannon produces a hollow roar of wind, but no blast. It is powered by anti-matter, and as long as you keep the ray-projector trained on him it cannot function.

'No problem,' growls MEGATRON. 'I can quite adequately crush you with my bare hands. Perhaps that will be more enjoyable –'

He is just reaching down to seize you when the sound of tearing metal echoes through the room. The Auto-bots have found the hideout and are smashing their way in!

Turn to page **60**

You unroll the silvered foil. It is a perfect mirror-surface, and that gives you an idea. Using a stick of bubble-gum from your pocket, you tack the foil to the inside of the cupboard door like a poster. Then you fling the door open. In their triumph, the Decepticons had forgotten all about you. They react with astonishment, but for MEGATRON battle is a reflex action. He raises his arm-cannon instinctively and unleashes a tremendous burst of fusion energy – *straight at you.*

But your plan works, because MEGATRON fires at where he thinks you're standing, but actually hits your reflected image in the mirror-foil. You duck back and shield your face from the heat of the blast, which rips the cupboard door off its hinges and sends it crashing into RUMBLE with stunning force. You are very satisfied to hear RUMBLE's groan as he struggles to recover.

'Foolish human,' says MEGATRON with quiet menace. 'Your feeble trick only delays your death for an instant.' He moves around and aims his cannon straight into the cupboard where you are hiding. For a moment it seems that nothing can save you, but then you hear the sound of the outer door being smashed in.

'The Autobots!' say you and MEGATRON together.

Turn to page **57**

You are in the cell for hours. RUMBLE does not return. He must have forgotten all about you, because you hear him scurrying around to MEGATRON's impatient orders. At last the Decepticons leave, turning out all the lights as they go and plunging you into total darkness.

You cannot tell how long you have been waiting, but finally there is a glimmer of light. Heavy metal footsteps approach your cell. Is it RUMBLE, returning to finish you off? No, a different robot appears. He is gleaming white and black: PROWL, one of the Autobots.

'Soon have you out of there,' says PROWL, his massive strength bending the bars like wire. 'The Decepticons got away with the vital microchips they were after, but at least no-one was killed.'

You hope that the Autobots will be able to find MEGATRON and stop his evil plans. But your own part in the adventure has reached

THE END

The mighty robots grapple, each pounding the other with blows that could shatter rock. All you can do is watch helplessly. The clanging punches ring out across the heath. Blasts of laser-light and crackling anti-matter energy burn the ground. At one moment MEGATRON seems to be getting the upper hand. He has forced OPTIMUS to the ground and is about to deliver a crushing cannon-shot, but the Autobot leader rolls aside at the last moment, catching his foe's leg in a steel grip and upending him with a titanic heave.

Before MEGATRON can recover, OPTIMUS seizes him and lifts him up into the air, then sends him crashing against the Druid Stone. The impact must have damaged MEGATRON's arm, because it hangs limply by his side as he gets up. 'Curse you, OPTIMUS!' he snarls, waving his other fist. 'We shall meet another day, and then I shall be the victor.' With that he disappears.

RUMBLE whines as he sees his master abandoning him, but PROWL has him pinned fast. OPTIMUS laughs, placing his huge metal hand on your shoulder. 'MEGATRON will not bother anyone for a while, as he will need repairs. We have recovered the microchips and captured RUMBLE. None of this could have been achieved without your help, my Earth friend.'

You cannot help grinning with pride!

THE END

You have never been so relieved to see anyone in your life. OPTIMUS PRIME stomps into the control room, effortlessly sweeping aside a girder that the enraged MEGATRON hurls at him. He delivers a bolt of laser-power to stop RUMBLE from getting to his feet, then charges at MEGATRON himself.

Turn to page **66**

While their backs are turned, you sneak past the Decepticons and hide yourself in a cupboard. Pausing only to check that there is a handle on the inside so you can get out again, you pull the door shut. You put your ear to the door and strain to catch what the Decepticons are talking about. But then you hear RUMBLE's footsteps approaching your hiding-place! For a moment you think he must have spotted you, that he is about to wrench open the cupboard door and drag you out . . . But he just stands nearby and starts to examine the microchips they stole from the convoy.

As your eyes adjust to the faint glimmer of light that is coming under the cupboard door, you notice that you are in some sort of storeroom. Several items are here, and maybe you can use one of them against the Decepticons. Which will you try:

A boxful of ball bearings? Turn to page **49**
An 'anti-matter' ray projector? Turn to page **50**
A sheet of silvered foil? Turn to page **51**

You move quickly but quietly to the outer door. As you run up the ramp, it swings back automatically and you emerge into the sunlight and fresh air. You see the huge form of OPTIMUS PRIME, the Autobot leader, some distance away, obviously searching for some sign of where the Decepticons went with their stolen haul. His keen sensors detect you at once when you start to wave at him, and he rushes over to where you are pointing.

The Decepticons must have heard the door opening, because they come out of their hideout. RUMBLE has a nasty look in his eye as he says, 'Meddlesome Earth-brat! You shall be the first to die.'

A powerful white fist sends RUMBLE spinning through the air before he can carry out his threat. 'There'll be no killing today, Decepticon,' says PROWL, hurling himself at his dazed foe.

You look up. Towering against the sky, OPTIMUS PRIME and MEGATRON face one another in wary silence. It is a showdown between titans!

Turn to page **56**

OPTIMUS PRIME enters the control room, and you have never been so relieved to see anyone in your life. MEGATRON raises his deadly cannon, but you react quickly by bathing him in the light of the ray-projector so that he cannot use it. MEGATRON curses you for interfering, but OPTIMUS says, 'Surely it's only fair, MEGATRON. You have your ally, and I have mine.' Glancing at RUMBLE as he speaks, the Autobot leader delivers a bolt of laser-power to stun the smaller robot. Then he charges at MEGATRON.

Turn to page **66**

You soon come to a side passage leading from the main corridor. Glancing at symbols on the walls, OPTIMUS tells you that it leads to the generators that supply power to the computers in the hideout.

*If you think it would be worth trying to sabotage the generators, turn to page **64***
*If you think it's more important to find the Decepticons quickly, turn to page **62***

You creep along the silent corridor. You are surprised how quietly OPTIMUS PRIME can move in spite of his huge size. Through a loose grating in the wall you can hear tinny voices. It is too small for OPTIMUS, but he prises it back so that you can crawl through. You find yourself looking out across the Decepticons' control room. MEGATRON is examining the microchips while RUMBLE gathers various items together and packs them into boxes.

'It looks as if they're getting ready to leave here,' you whisper to OPTIMUS after wriggling back through the grating to join him.

'Not if I can help it!' he replies. He turns and walks back along the corridor, searching for the way to the control room, and you have to run to keep up with his determined stride.

Turn to page **63**

You soon reach the master control room. It is the nerve centre of MEGATRON's hideout – the centre of his web. RUMBLE and MEGATRON have their backs to you, eagerly poring over the priceless electronic components they have stolen.

'There's too much at stake to exactly play fair,' mutters OPTIMUS PRIME. He aims his laser and sends a blinding burst of energy through the air into RUMBLE. The blast takes the bullying little robot unawares and sends him flying into a computer unit, stunned.

'OPTIMUS!' shouts MEGATRON, turning to behold his dearest foe. 'This will be our last battle, Autobot –'

OPTIMUS charges forward to attack him. 'You may be right about that, MEGATRON,' he says grimly.

Turn to page **66**

With OPTIMUS PRIME just ahead of you, you make your way down to the thundering generators. You stand in front of tall pylons that flicker with electricity and a fusion generator that produces the millions of watts of power MEGATRON needs for his weapons and alien devices.

Just as OPTIMUS is about to step forward and start disconnecting the cables leading from the generator, it starts to shut down of its own accord. Looking back in alarm, you see the lights in the corridor going out.

'They're leaving,' cries OPTIMUS – 'abandoning the hideout!' He runs back along the corridor, but it is too late. You can hear the sound of screeching jets carrying away the Decepticons and their stolen cargo. There is no chance of catching them now.

Turn to page **65**

All you can do is watch helplessly as the metal titans pound one another with clanging blows. Each punch could smash a stone wall, but neither seems to be getting the upper hand. Seeing the crate of microchips that the Decepticons stole, you race forward and pull off the lid. The delicate components are stored carefully within. MEGATRON notices you out of the corner of his eye and turns, alarmed that you will damage the microchips. This distraction is just the advantage that OPTIMUS has been waiting for. He delivers a stunning blow that throws MEGATRON back into the computer panels. There is a sizzling flash of electricity and MEGATRON, damaged, makes for a secret exit. RUMBLE has also recovered and, seeing his evil master defeated, slinks along to make his escape also.

'Let them go!' laughs OPTIMUS, placing his huge metal hand on your shoulder. 'They will do no harm for a while, and we have recovered the microchips they stole. You played a great part in this victory, my Earth friend.'

You cannot help grinning with pride!

THE END

THE TRANSFORMERS™: DINOBOT WAR
by Dave Morris

Robot Dinosaurs!

Earth has been invaded by the powerful robots from the distant plant Cybertron – the Heroic Autobots and their enemies, the Evil Decepticons. They can disguise their robot shapes as earthly machines and transform for battle at lightning speed. The battle between Good and Evil rages on Earth . . .

You are the hero of this book – suddenly you are thrust into the deadly struggle. With the help of secret devices, found on an ancient flying saucer, you could travel back to prehistoric times and help the Heroic Dinobots in their battle against the Evil Decepticons.

If you dare . . .

If you collect Transformers™, this book is for you!

SBN 0 0552 523143

THE TRANSFORMERS™
PERIL FROM THE STARS
by Dave Morris

Evil Robots walk among us!

Earth has been invaded by the powerful robots from the distant planet Cybertron – the Heroic Autobots and their enemies, the Evil Decepticons. They can disguise their robot shapes as earthly machines and transform for battle at lightning speed. The battle between Good and Evil rages on Earth . . .

You are the hero of this book – suddenly you are thrust into the deadly struggle

You will meet the valiant Autobot JAZZ and help him fight against the evil STARSCREAM. But be careful – your actions will decide whether the Decepticon is defeated or whether he gets the terrible weapons he needs to overthrow the world!

If you collect Transformers™, this book is for you!

SBN 0 552 523151

THE TRANSFORMERS™: ISLAND OF FEAR
by Dave Morris

Earth has been invaded by the powerful robots from the distant planet Cybertron – the Heroic Autobots and their enemies, the Evil Decepticons. They can disguise their robot shapes as earthly machines and transform for battle at lightning speed. The battle between Good and Evil rages on Earth . . .

You are the hero of this book – suddenly you are thrust into the deadly struggle.

An exotic holiday island is terrorized by the murderous DIRGE. Brave BEACHCOMBER, a Heroic Autobot, needs your help to combat the Decepticon's menacing schemes. But the price of failure is death!

If you collect Transformers™, this book is for you!

SBN 0 552 52316X

T.R. BEAR

ENTER T.R.
by Terrance Dicks

It all started when Jimmy got a parcel from his Uncle Colin in America. The teddy bear inside was unlike any bear Jimmy had ever seen. He looked tough, and he was wearing glasses! According to the label, his name was Theodore Roosevelt — T.R. for short.

Jimmy soon finds out that life with T.R. Bear is quite eventful . . .

0 552 52301 1

T.R. GOES TO SCHOOL
by Terrance Dicks

"You won't hear a peep out of me, kid," promises T.R. Bear when Jimmy decides to take him to school for show and tell. The trouble is that T.R. is a rather excitable bear and tends to break the rules.

T.R.'s visit to school turns out to be a day that Jimmy would never forget!

0 552 52302 X

If you would like to receive a Newsletter about our new Children's books, just fill in the coupon below with your name and address (or copy it on to a separate piece of paper if you don't want to spoil your book) and send it to:

THE CHILDREN'S BOOKS EDITOR
YOUNG CORGI BOOKS
61-63 UXBRIDGE ROAD
EALING
LONDON W5 5SA

Please send me a Children's Newsletter:

Name: ....

Address: ....

....

....

All the books on the previous pages are available at your local bookshop or can be ordered direct from the publishers: Cash Sales Dept., Transworld Publishers Ltd., 61-63 Uxbridge Road, Ealing, London W5 5SA.

Please enclose the cost of the book(s), together with the following for postage and packing costs:

Orders up to a value of £5.00   50p
Orders of a value over £5.00   Free

Please note that payment should be made by cheque or postal order in £ sterling.